101 Things Young Man Every ~~Boy~~ of Color Should Know

Also by LaMarr Darnell Shields

Dare to Be Queen

Rhyme and Reason: A Hip Hop Tool for the Classroom

Hands Off: Strategies to Combat Youth Violence

10 Steps Out of Puberty

El Primer Dia De La Escuela (The First Day of School)

Poems for the Oppressed

"At a time when many young men of color face uncertainty and lack of guidance, this book offers what is missing. The collection of advice composed by LaMarr Darnell Shields offers a blueprint that if absorbed accordingly will allow its readers to navigate a world that can seem overwhelming and lonely at times."

-NICK FIGUEROA, M.ED., Dean of Undergraduate Admission, Framingham State College

If you have been following the writings and work of Brother LaMarr Darnell Shields, then you know of his profound love for Black boys; you know of his passion to rescue Black boys; you know that he is on a mission to give voice to those precious young boys that are valued the least and that far too many policy-makers have forgotten; and, you come to know, respect and appreciate his generous spirit and unyielding commitment to helping Black boys find purpose and meaning in their lives. In *101 Things Every Boy/Young Man of Color Should Know*, Brother Shields has given Black men an opportunity to edify, affirm, teach, encourage, inspire, guide and connect with Black boys. His book is truly a wonderful and special gift to Black boys, and will help all those that read it to never, never give up and to keep their eyes on the prize.

-RICHARD A. ROWE, President / CEO, African American Male Leadership Institute

2009 by LaMarr Darnell Shields

ISBN 978-0-9659028-6-1

For information address: Hotep Press, 2437 Maryland Avenue, Baltimore, Maryland 21218

Acknowledgements

101 Things Every Boy/Young Man of Color Should Know owes its existence to boys of color all over the world who have a struggled against racism, poverty, violence, legal status, labels, and academic challenges. Whatever position you find yourself in today, I pray that this book will serve as an inspiration and guide to give you the push that we all need at times.

101 Things Every Boy/Young Man of Color Should Know is dedicated to my son Mosiah Sekou Samuel Shields, and my nephews, Jonel, Pierre, Phil, Jordan, and Jahi. To the Paul Robeson Academic International School of Excellence Scholars, the Bluford Drew Jemison Academy and the Bronx Eagle Academy student bodies, thank you for allowing me to share my experiences with you. Scott Johnson, I appreciate you. To the best business partner in the world, David Miller-- your commitment to boys of color is undeniable. The brothers of Morehouse College, continue being the fine examples of manhood that you are. Tupac and Biggie Smalls – thanks for the inspiration. A mis hermanos Latinos, muchisimas gracias. To all the men who poured into my spirit, especially my father John H. Shields and my mentor from Grambling Señor Brooks, you taught me to pay it forward. To my KAOS brothers, who gave me many stories over the years, much respect. Curits, Andre, Karoy, and Derick, may you RIP.

To the media genius, Janks Morton, who within a few weeks, put this book on the silver screen, and created a national dialogue about boys of color while at the same time giving voice to the pages that screamed at me daily, you're simply the best. To an awesome production crew who worked diligently on the documentary Men to Boys – I appreciate your dedication to my vision. My first child, Monique, Kim aka Tootie, Kobie, and Anthony – I carry your lessons with me. To the men and women who contributed to this project: Lamar Tyler, Brandon Whitney, Kaushik Iyer, Kevin Brooks, Keon Gerow, Gerald Thomas, Jamal Munnerlyn, Bomani, Richard Rowe, Omar Muhhamad, Yolanda Abel, Cheria Dial, Sandy Mason, and Kobie Kiambu -- thank you for your words. And to an awesome pastor and friend, Willie F. Wilson it is your framework for boys and young men of color that served as the road map for this project. Last but not least, to President Obama, all I can say is thank you for stepping up to the plate and showing boys of color all over the world a true example of manhood.

Foreword

Young Brother,

I want you to know how to KISS as you go through life. In case you haven't heard of the KISS before, it means Keep It Simple, Stupid. Remember to Keep It Simple as life hands you one choice after another that defines who you are and what you can accomplish, and you will limit the number of times when you wind up feeling -- and being -- Stupid. Whether the choices you make in life involve your education, career or personal relationships, you will often find that in some way it will help to Keep It Simple.

Believe it or not, once you are enrolled in school it is simpler to stay in and finish than to drop out. I know school can be challenging and there can be events outside of the classroom that make it hard for you to stay, but more education brings more opportunities. You never know when your ability to speak well, write clear sentences and reach thoughtful conclusions will serve you. These are all skills that you get and fine tune in school, and you'd have a hard time finding anyone who runs anything that doesn't have these skills. Whether they're in business for themselves or a corporation, a non-profit agency or a government office, it was education that got them there. Many people who are doing well in the street economy naturally possess significant skills. Just think of what they could be running with a college degree! Besides, if you drop out and promise yourself you'll go back, you never know what will happen between your point of decision and the always uncertain future. You can't control everything in life, but taking control of your education is simple.

Career success is not simple, but getting on the path to it is. Decide what you want to achieve, learn all you can about it and commit to working hard to get it. Three simple steps, but they're not easy. I remember when I was deciding whether to run for Congress. Many people, including my famous father, were not 100% behind my decision. But my mind was made up. I learned more about Congress, my congressional district and campaigning, then I launched into the hardest work I've ever done. People talked about me, followed me everywhere and I went days without rest. There were times when I hated the pressure, but I knew I could do a lot of good as a Member of Congress. With the help of friends and supporters, I stayed strong and won that first campaign in 1995 and every one of my campaigns since.

Personal relationships can make you crazier than anything, but here again the KISS rule can apply. If you're juggling several partners, that's not keeping it simple. If you're not happy in your relationship and all you're doing about that is picking fights with your partner, you're not keeping it simple. If you're not parenting your children, you're not keeping it simple. There are thousands of books and experts available to help you with your relationship. The simplest thing to do is to use as many as you can. They're just tools, and a man never hesitates to use the tools he needs to get the results he wants.

This book is a very useful tool. Read it. It's filled with information that will help you remember to KISS, and everyone wants to be a good KISSer.

- Congressman Jesse L. Jackson, Jr. (D-IL)

Introduction

Make no mistake about it – our young men are in a state of crisis. Too few African-American males graduate from high school and far too many are incarcerated. A college education remains elusive while unemployment and under-employment are available in abundance. Yes, the statistics are frightening but our community must not remain frozen by fear. The crisis within our community is a thundering call to action. Our young men need us.

Academic theories, studies, and hypotheses are useful in identifying the turmoil but they won't solve the problem. Only we, as a community, can truly implement the strategies that will equip our young men with the confidence, knowledge, and tools that they need to defy the statistics and claim their place in society as successful and capable men. *101 Things Every Boy/Young Man of Color Should Know* is a valuable tool in an overall plan to address the myriad of challenges facing our young men.

As the Founding Principal of the Eagle Academy for Young Men in New York City and now as President of the Eagle Academy Foundation, I have witnessed the overwhelming need for our young men to not only receive a quality education but also their potent emotional desire to feel valued and cared for. Too many young people believe that adults simply don't care about their challenges. They want to know that we, individually and as a community, care enough to pay attention and that we haven't counted them out. *101 Things Every Boy/Young Man of Color Should Know* sends a powerful message to our young men. Yes, we care. Yes, we are here to help you. Yes, we believe you. Yes, young men, you can count on us.

As an advocate and creator of mentoring programs, I know that young men respond positively when adult men open up the lines of communication. Yes, as adults we need to alert our young men when they are making mistakes but, just as importantly, we must relay knowledge so that our young men can succeed. We must recognize their achievements and encourage them to keep striving.

101 Things Every Boy/Young Man of Color Should Know provides a magnificent way to improve the lines of communication between us and our young men. This book is not just a must-read for every young man but for men, women, parents, caretakers, educators, and everyone who wants to improve the lives of our male youth.

Young men, this book is for you. Whether or not you have an adult male in your life, let *101 Things Every Boy/Young Man of Color Should Know* be a constant reminder of how much you are cherished and valued by your community. Take encouragement from these words. As men, we all have choices to make. Some choices are relatively simple but others can be difficult. Let this book be a guide when you are looking for advice on how to make decisions in your life. Share these words with your friends. Read them and re-read them. Incorporate the book's advice into your life and you will see that the possibilities are endless. As a successful adult male it will then be your responsibility to propel this movement forward and share *101 Things Every Boy/Young Man of Color Should Know* with the youth in your community. This book may seem modest but don't underestimate the power of words. These 101 things will make a powerful impact in your life.

Yours in the struggle,

David C. Banks

Man, listen up!

When I was a young boy growing up in Chicago, I knew not to step out of line no matter how far from home I was. I could be two, three blocks from my house and there would always be someone who knew my mother, father, grandparents or older siblings standing watch and yelling "You know better, LaMarr Darnell Shields!" if I did something wrong.

Sadly, that sense of community and collective responsibility is currently missing from the childhoods of many boys of color - and it's having a terrible effect on you and your friends.

Boys need and want advice on all kinds of issues, for all kinds of problems, questions, and concerns. Often, you don't know who or how to ask, and it seems that most self-help books are written for girls.

Well, this book, *101 Things Every Boy/Young Man of Color Should Know* is written especially for you. You can be 9 or 99. It doesn't matter. I designed this book to help you grow and develop into a strong, responsible man. Moreover, I wrote *101 Things Every Boy/Young Man of Color Should Know* because there are some things men must share with you that we feel will help you deal with some of the problems you will encounter on your road to manhood. A lot of older men I know tell me they wished they would have listened to the advice they received from other men when they were younger. Other men tell me that they didn't grow up with a man in their life who could share words of wisdom. Sadly, too many men of color are now in prison, dead, or facing other consequences for being hard-headed or not having access to GOOD advice when they were growing up.

So this book was written for you out of a sense of urgency. We have allowed you to go without adequate schooling, health care, emotional support, or community leadership for too long. As a result you have sunk deeper into crisis..

Boys and young men of color make up 40% of the U.S. population under the age of 25. Public systems ought to be tailored to meet their needs. Public services should be wrought with opportunities and paths that ensure the success of boys and men of color. However, startling statistics from The Centers for Disease Control and Prevention about poor health and less than desirable social outcomes paint a bleak picture for the future of boys and young men of color:

- Minority youth make up 23% of total population ages 10-17 but constitute 52% of incarcerated youth. And whether innocent or guilty, a majority of youth of color will have been arrested before the age of 21.

- Boys and young men of color under age 25 represent approximately 67% of the diagnosed HIV positive cases as since the beginning of the AIDS epidemic.

- 40% of African American men and 37% of Latino men in the U.S. die prematurely compared to 21% of white men.

- Male students are consistently less likely than their female counterparts to graduate from high school. While 57.8% percent of Black female students graduate, that's true for only 44.3% of Black males. For Latinos, the female and male graduation figures are 59.9% and 50.1% respectively.

Despite these grim statistics, there are still many young men who are graduating from high school, going to college, not in prison, taking care of their children, and not selling or using drugs. This book is for those young men, as well as for the ones who have fallen through the cracks and are working hard to get back on track.

There are a lot of things you know, but there are a whole lot of things you don't know. So I took it upon myself to ask other men and women of color the following question: "What do boys or young men of color need to know?" What I found from talking to these ordinary men and women, were extraordinary treasures; and you are holding the jewels in your hands. This is our way of saying that we love you. And if you never hear it again, you know that the men and women who contributed to this book truly do.

We know it is not easy being a boy of color, but we hope that this book will inspire and motivate you to succeed despite of what people might say or think about you. This book is full of GOOD advice that will definitely help you transition from boyhood to manhood but my favorite quote of them all is Know that guilt is a wasted emotion.

Enjoy!
LaMarr Darnell Shields
(The little boy from the south side of Chicago)

A Legacy of Lessons

It's your time to be the best,
Give it your all then you can rest.
Learn from those who laid the foundation,
It's your time to build a nation.
Barack said it best, "Yes, you can!"
Daddy might not be there, so be your own man.
Look at the greats that came before,
Malcolm, Marcus, Martin, and so many more.
Langston wrote, and Jesse ran
Muhammad Ali fought with his mind and hands
Dr. Ben and Clarke made our story no mystery
While Dr. Carson's brain surgery made history.
James Farmer was a great debater. Al Sharpton came much later.
Reginald F. Lewis made tons of money,
Richard Pryor was oh so funny.
Nelson Mandela was freed from jail, while Cinque the African set sail.
Paul Robeson perfected prose and plays,
Minister Farrakhan focuses on freedom, today.
Bob Johnson gave us BET, and Thurgood Marshall fought for our civil liberties.
The Duke and Dizzy made all that Jazz,
While Bill Cosby turned from laughs to dads.
Tupac and Biggie rapped from the heart,
WEB DuBois and Booker T were known to be smart,
While Alvin Ailey, Basqiat, and Bearden perfected their art.
No matter the name,
No matter the profession,
Men of color provide a universal lesson of expression.

It is easier to build strong children than to repair broken men.

-Frederick Douglass

Know that you have the potential to be **great**; YES YOU CAN/SI SE PUEDE!!!

no.1

Know that every **choice** you make **has a** **consequence** tied to it.

no.2

Know that **racism does exist**, but never use it as an excuse to fail.

no.3

Know that your **net worth** does not determine your **self-worth**.

no.4

Know that **failure** is a lesson and not the end.

no.5

Know the lesson in **losing**.

no.6

Know the difference between **no** and **never** so that you can **always** bounce back from rejection. no.7

Know **how to** walk away.

Know the **power** of your words.

no. 9

Know the **power** of your thoughts.

no. 10

Know **your history** and never forget your ancestors.

no.11

Know that **no** one **owes** you anything.

no.12

Know the **consequences** of unprotected sex.

no.13

Know that *you* are not a **nigga**!

no.14

Know the
importance of
time.

no.15

Know how to **shine** your own **shoes**.

no.16

Know how
to **accept**
criticism.

no.17

Know how to enjoy **life.**

Know how to **admit** when you are wrong.

no.19

Know how to
rest.

no.20

Know how to give and **receive** a compliment.

no.21

Know a **little**
bit about **a lot**
of things.

no.22

Know that *your*
past doesn't
dictate *your*
future.

no.23

Know **how** to
tie a tie.

Know the **value** of **prayer** and meditation.

Know what to **do**
when stopped
by the **police**.

no.26

Know when to be still or **quiet**.

no.27

Know when to **speak up**.

no.28

Know the meaning of your **name**.

no.29

Know how to **ask** questions properly.

Know the
importance
of **listening**
(to your inner voice).

no.31

Know how to **place** and **use** table settings.

Know how **to** tip.

Know how to sew buttons.

Know the
power of
choice.

no.35

Know the
importance
of friendship.

no.36

Know that every life is **sacred** and precious.

Know how
to get
organized.

no.38

Know that being healthy emotionally, **mentally** and physically is **critical** to your success.

no.39

Know that it is
ok to cry.

no.40

Know that your **skin** color does not determine your destiny.

no.41

Know that **first** impressions are lasting.

no.42

Know the importance of **honoring** your word.

no.43

Know how to speak at **one** **language** other than your native tongue.

Know how to
communicate
your feelings.

no.45

Know that guilt
is a **wasted**
emotion.

no.46

Know that you
are **loved**.

no.47

Know how to **cook**.

Know that the word **minority** should never determine your status.

no.49

Know the **value** of having a **good** work ethic.

Know how to be humble.

no.51

Know how to pick your **friends**; you will often be judged by the **company** that you keep.

Know that **character** opens doors **that** intellect cannot.

no.53

Know that you are the **only** one that can **block** your blessings.

no.54

Know that when you **forgive**, you free yourself from bondage.

no.55

Know that there are a million ways to make **money** that are easier than playing professional sports or **rapping**.

no.56

Know that you have the ability to be a **great** father even if you didn't have one.

no.57

Know that having manners and speaking **grammatically correct** is not "acting white".

no.58

Know the **importance** of managing your **credit**.

no.59

Know that everyone is **not** out to get you.

no.60

Know the importance of a **genuine** smile.

no.61

Know how to **care** for those **less** fortunate than **you**.

no.62

Know how to use
a **power** tool
correctly.

no.63

Know how to **ask** for emotional support.

no.64

Know how to appreciate **Ramen Noodles**.

no.65

Know the importance of holding your **head high**, shaking hands **firmly** and **walking** purposefully.

no.66

Know how to hold your **mate's** hand.

no.67

Know how to temper your temperament.

no.68

Know how to **give** more than you take.

no.69

Know how to **forgive** your parents.

no. 70

Know that it is **Ok**
to **stand alone**,
if you are standing
for the **right**
principles.

no.71

Know that just because you **may** have been born on the **wrong side** of the tracks, don't mean you can't

no. 72 crossover.

Know that your current **situation** does not predict your future circumstances.

no.73

Know that if you don't know and **love** yourself, it will be impossible to genuinely love anyone else.

no. 74

Know that your
education
is the **highest**
"street cred"
you will ever
obtain. no.75

Know that **impossible** doesn't exist...... So Dream On.

no.76

Know how to **use** sports.....as **opposed to** letting sports use you.

no.77

Know that it is **ok** to **show** your emotions........ cry, laugh, and **love**.

no.78

Know that it is quite **possible** to be **confident** and humble at the same time.

no. 79

Know that **hard** **work** really does **pay off.**

no.80

Know that **smart** people learn from other's mistakes, so **listen** **and** pay attention.

no.81

Know that **peer** pressure only exists if you don't know **who** you are and what you want out of **life**.

no.82

Know that you will be **called** certain things in life but it's what you answer to that's **important.**

no.83

Know that your integrity and **character** will definitely be called into question at some point.

no.84

Know that saying I didn't have a **relationship** with my father is no longer a valid excuse for not being productive or successful. no.85

Know and understand your **history**, so that you will have a better sense of your **obligations** and purpose.

no.86

Know that fatherhood, **children** and **family** are blessings, and your only true legacy; make sure you **value** them above everything else.

no.87

Know that respect is **earned** so be sure to lead by example.

no.88

Know that our **women** must always be loved, respected, and protected.

no.89

Know that you must do everything possible to make your **family**, community and people proud of you.

no.90

Know that
the **price** of
freedom is
responsibility.

no.91

Know how to **ask**

someone **on a**

date.

Know how to avoid **conflict** when you don't like the person that your mother is in **love** with.

no.93

Know how to choose the **right** haircut to fit your purpose and **personality**.

no.94

Know the **proper** attire to wear to a job interview.

Know when and how to shave.

Know how to **change** the oil in a car.

no.97

Know when
you are being
disrespected and
when you are being
disrespectful.

no.98

Know how to **effectively** communicate **with** all people.

no.99

Know how to **refrain** from **underestimating** your ability to **influence** others.

no.100

Know that **mediocrity** must always take a back seat to excellence.

no. 101

January 15, 2007

Dear Mr. Shields,

I am a sixteen-year old high school student. Last year, you spoke to our entire student body about the challenges you were faced with as a young boy growing up in Chicago. You talked about your best friend being killed, being kicked out of school, and not being the best student in class. All the things that I can relate to. But what made me pay attention the most, was when you said that you never once blamed anyone for what happened to you.

Mr. Shields, my entire life, I have always blamed my father for not providing me with, as you said in your speech, an "emotional vocabulary". So I did like all my boys did, I attempted to fight my way out of my situation, and ended up a juvenile delinquent. Even though you were talking to the entire school, it was like you were in my head. I hate when people get in my head!

I know now, that even though my dad is not in my life, I thank God for people like you who still embrace boys like me, even when we seem like we don't want to be embraced. Many of us don't know how to relate to men, because we were raised by women. I guess that's what happens when all the men roll out.

Anyway, your speech was tight. You talked about the power of words. And how they can be used to heal or kill. Throughout my life, I have been told that I wasn't going to make it. And I really believed them until you told us that we can rewrite our own story.

On another note, I still think Lil Wayne is better than Jay-Z.

Thanks for coming to my school.

Sincerely,

Martin Jackson

About the Author

Outspoken, Insightful, Visionary, Compassionate, Innovative, Youthful, Funny, Precocious, and Charismatic are some of the ways LaMarr Darnell Shields, the co-founder and president of the Urban Leadership Institute has been described. As a rising star amongst his peers, LaMarr has been featured in numerous media outlets for his achievements in the education and motivation of young people. Before Urban Leadership Institute, Shields taught at the third oldest high school in the country, lived in Latin America, spoke at the White House, wrote several books and articles, founded the Paul Robeson Academic International School of Excellence (PRAISE), hosted a teen television show, and taught at the prestigious Johns Hopkins University.

When asked about his passion, Shields says that he owes it to all the teachers he drove to an early retirement. Because of them, Shields says adults have to be creative when helping young people become successful.

While his accomplishments are commendable, it is important to note that due to his poor academic performance and mischievous behavior in school, LaMarr Darnell Shields was not expected to succeed. While in the 11th grade, he was expelled. However, after searching dozens of high schools and receiving numerous rejections, due to his defiant background and failing grades, he was fortunate to get accepted into another high school, and later became an honor roll student, then a distinguished graduate of Grambling State University and La Universidad de Coahuila in Mexico, where he majored in Political Science and Spanish. After acquiring his undergraduate degree, he went on to earn a Masters Degree in Education from Loyola College of Maryland.

But most of his education has come from hardships and personal tragedies. At a young age, Shields lost three of his closest friends to violence. "I've found that sometimes the very thing that has hurt you the most, is the very thing you can use to help others," says Shields.

LaMarr doesn't live in the past but uses those experiences to guide others to a more positive future filled with possibilities. "I am who I am today because I chose to take advantage of opportunities given to me," says LaMarr. "If you don't identify who you are, others will."

LaMarr is the proud Baba (father) to Hadiya, Sameera, and Mosiah Shields, as well as a loving husband to Comedienne Meshelle.

Books by other great men of Color

Dare to Be King – David C. Miller
The Black Male Handbook: A Blueprint for Life - Kevin Powell
Invisible Man - Ralph Ellison
Hunger of Memory: The Education of Richard Rodriguez - Richard Rodriguez
Native Son - Richard Wright
A Lesson Before Dying - Earnest Gaines
The Autobiography of Malcolm X - Alex Hailey
Makes Me Wanna Holler: A Young Black Man in America - Nathan McCall
Things Fall Apart - Chinua Achebe
The Souls of Black Folk - W.E.B. DuBois
The Fire Next Time - James Baldwin
*Black Men, Obsolete, Single, Dangerous?: The Afrikan American Family in
Transition* –Haki Madhubuti
Billy - Albert French
Manchild in the Promised Land - Claude Brown
Black Boy - Richard Wright
The Color of Water: A Black Man's Tribute to His White Mother - James McBride
Letters to a Young Brother - Hill Harper
Down This Mean Street - Piri Thomas
Always Running: La Vida Loca: Gang Days in L.A. - Luis J. Rodriguez

Men II Boys

To order copies of the documentary

Men to Boys,

the companion to

101 Things Every Boy/Young Man of Color Should Know

please visit www.mentoboys.com.